Reaching for Honey

Books by Carolyn Stoloff:

Stepping Out
Unicorn Press
In the Red Meadow
New Rivers Press (chapbook)
Dying to Survive
Doubleday and Company
Lighter-Than-Night Verse
Red Hill Press (chapbook)
Swiftly Now
Ohio University Press
A Spool of Blue, New and Selected Poems
Poets Now series, Scarecrow Press
You Came to Meet Someone Else
Asylum Arts Press
Greatest Hits (chapbook)
Pudding House Publications

Reaching for Honey

poetry by

Carolyn Stoloff

Red Hen Press *Los Angeles 2004*

Front cover art *Regret* by Giselle Gautreau
Back cover bee image used by permission of CEOS University of Bath UK
Author photo in Taos, New Mexico by Sonya Hess

Book design by: James M. Harmon
Cover Design by: Mark E. Cull

First Edition
ISBN 1-888996-57-9
Library of Congress Catalog Card Number: 2003098413

The City of Los Angeles Cultural Affairs Department, California Arts Council and the Los Angeles County Arts Commission partially support Red Hen Press.

Red Hen Press
www.redhen.org

First Edition

Acknowledgments

The author thanks the editors of the following publications in which these poems first appeared (sometimes in an earlier version):

ACM: "Sleep Is the Place With No Knobs"; *The Agni Review:* "Letter from Connecticut" (as "Letter from Dick"); *The Bridge:* "Down the Hall, the Bookman," "Between Home and Home"; *Caliban*: "Bulletins From Your Early Morning News Center," "Night's Drownings and Resuscitations," "Short Story"; *The Chariton Review*: "Alive," "The Iron Era of Trains Returns"; *Contact II*: "The Redon Boy," "Emptying the Bowl"; *The Current*: "It's Always Then Now"; *Embers*: "On the Long Fall Down the Vault Steps Stopped"; *The Glass Cherry*: "The White Hour"; *Hanging Loose*: "What I Wish, What I Want"; *Hubbub*: "Taking Off" (Vi Gale Award, 1999); *Images*: "Communing with Myself," "Moon's Wife"; *Invisible City*: "Close Call," "To Be Borne Again"; *The Little Magazine*: "In the Absence of Anyone"; *Malahat Review*: "February 8"; *Manhattan Review*: "Nelson the Mailman," "You Don't Hear Me"; *Neovictorian/ Cochlea*: "Elegy"; *Oasis*: "With Your Breath"; *Open Unison Stop*: "A Snowflake in the Eye"; *Paintbrush*: "A Wilderness in the Veins," "Offering," "Master Fashioner"; *Partisan Review*: "Letter from Indiana"; *Poet Lore*: "Is There Another Fruit"; *Poetry New York*: "Winter Morning"; *Poetry Northwest*: "Behind the Old Woman's Dark Glasses" (as "The Countess"), "The Innermost Room," "At the Bottom of the Box"; *The Signal*: "Evening with an Hourglass," "In a Museum of Contemporary Art"; *The Southern Poetry Review*: "Widow Road," "The Headlight Through Us"; *The Southern Review*: "Anticipating the End Of Distance"; *Syn/aes/the/tic*: "When Asked How This Drawing Series Began, He Said:"; *Talisman*: "As Long As I Live," "I Hear Longing Strings," "Stopping the Arrow to Weigh Its Flight," "Tasting The Stuff of Clouds," "Your Path To Perspective"; *Taos Review*: "Mourning Raga for Hannah Tillich"; *West Branch*: "Sketch of Tilli"; *Yefief*: "Untitled."

The following poems were reprinted in *New Directions,* Volume 53: "February 8," "On the Long Fall Down the Vault Steps Stopped," "Close Call."

Epigraph part IV, page 133, *Sonnets To Orpheus,* The Norton Library. Rilke's reply to a questionnaire from his polish translator, Witold von Hulewicz, November 13, 1925.

Table of Contents

III Time Shared

IV Reaching for Honey

To the memory of Kay Boyle,
friend and beacon

1. alive

Winter Morning

Manhattan

despite a northwind and predictions of sleet
dawn spreads in the theater of operations
where circling skaters incise ice
and twigs drop gauze over wounds
    in the lake's white back

stay with me
we'll climb snowheaps along the avenue
to watch lawyers race
    for the fast track to the Capitol
    where lobbyists with bowls
    of steaming oatmeal await them

above the square where union men gestured
just under the sky's low roof
cawing harpies harass the hawk who could kill
    them a pigeon for breakfast

below, near the flagpole
a boy stripped of his bright nylon armor
    sinks into snow like a violin

as the pall lightens over the Palisades
a red crane hoists a carved eagle
    from the coast of Lethe
    to a mast's pinnacle
from this aerie it sheds sawdust
    on the Hudson's crust

and there goes the judge's gold cufflink!
like a jet's lit window it assails
    the snow-flecked sky
as he instructs the jury to weigh
    the net's role
    in the case of the impaled butterfly

light spreads on evergreen corpses
    tossed every which way
    browning and shrinking
    half-buried at the hems of highrises
and on a statue without pedestal—centered
    in the school's cement court two teens
    fused by the heat of a wet kiss
    sway gently

as the light comes up—a lemon-tinged
    silver light—
joggers circle Washington's square
making prints but no sense
    on the fresh white skin of existence

Bulletins from Your Early Morning News Center

a janitor steps from a basement dragging something
    that thumps, something with knotted
    veins and potato eyes
and pitches it against a lamppost

on this tenth day of the strike, it's 72 degrees
forced to digest a silver pod with its tightly packed
    human peas, sky grumbles loudly

delays on Queens Boulevard into Manhattan
watch for a tractor-trailer accordion
    playing Dark Eyes in the left lane
and a large pile of pork

on the second floor of a brownstone
a seamstress, hemming at this early hour, bites
a thread as though day's wing were even now
    rushing the strident mistress of the dress
    to her threshold

showers and higher skirts predicted

but not the bullet that pierces an infant
    in her mother's arms
as her father proudly exhibits his new metal finger
    to a circle of tattooed males

past midnight, at the hour of departures, cyclists
    with smoking guns raged through a Long Island
    estate
toppling the hostess whose rights were instantly
    suppressed,
prompting one distinguished guest
    to vow to launch a world class trial

and what are you up to?

weighing bags under your eyes?
sweeping the pavement with your spread tail?
chewing a routine swallowed daily and baked afresh?

the 6:10 express has just left Penn Central
but no negotiations have been scheduled
and the mediator atop the engine rushes his mantra
    in order to dissolve before the first tunnel

The Iron Era of Trains Returns

coaches leaving the city line up to see
what the ones in front will see:
    puppets jiggling in windows
    as the city slips by,
perilously tilting back-porches,
purple asters each with a yellow eye

and a glimpse of the Hudson . . .
a few sails like tips of the hanky
    in grandpa's breast pocket

the w.c. is still locked
but the price of snacks rises
as the conductor thrusts his face close to mine

from under his moustache he sends little kisses
while punching small holes in my abdomen—
    that domain of bears and butterflies

a sulky child runs her finger along the ledge
    of her window and licks the dust

she won't notice yesteryear's dandruff
    on our padded shoulders
or guess our covert devices for draining wounds

it's time to change to winter oil!

you can tuck stress into the purse on your lap
    or a briefcase
but lust won't fit in the overhead bin

we gather together (seated, in rows)

stronger than experience, fantasy dissolves
    leaving no stain
so permits us our scapegoats, turkeys, whores,
    hunks and violins,

as, transported, we sit catching the intimate
    fish of reflection
through tinted windows

Alive

to Esteban Vicente, painter, the morning after the celebration of his 94th birthday

once again voice-boxes crackle and growl
caimans thrash in the steam pipes
an infant, mouth stuffed with a pear, is slipped
  into the oven in 5B
she should be tender in six hours
a roach accountant tallies the night's losses
  and records who has stopped, permanently,
  at which motels
but my ship glides faultlessly into its port of
  sheets, its voyage to Madagascar accomplished

the dream won't be shaved
round-eyed, ring-tailed citizens of the jungle,
caged without trial, begin to vanish in the hold
while on deck the customs inspector takes a few last
  puffs from his cigar

a minute peers from its hole and steps on to a
  branch in Central Park
there leaves hang from twigs like rock-climbers
  caught in crisis
naked feet pursued by fierce squirrels race around
  pedestals where bronze poets pose
the entire metropolis gyrates

and what about you, ancient philosopher,
what vistas have you collected in the pouches
  beneath your eyes?
show me your broad-brushed ochre and turquoise
  boulders of space
in the foreground a strand of blood comes into focus
as you wake
  wondering who's hammering tin in the blue morning,
as you wake, alive—
your head cradled on the white bosom of Day
that lusty woman who, night after night,
tows you past the cave of the octopus

Nelson the Mailman

we are the sheepish turning white masks
    toward you
across the creek

we are quick smiles stamped over each other,

seagulls you try to catch
    by waving your cap
when you've left your key in a lock

we are hidden receivers

our quivering antennae assess your progress
as you steer a sack packed with wind's
    contraband, door to door,

trailing your spoor—limp rubberbands

when night falls
when sidewalks submerge
    in the flood of sleep,
your sack escapes to soar above chimneys—
    black bloated demon
    with one malicious red eye—
snowing bills like confetti

wind snatches your cap

the blue corner-postbox drops its jaw
    coughing unaddressed resignations

a rolled report of gross earnings
won't fit
the stockholder's mail slot

but by day
when the taciturn plumber
crosses your path, snake in hand,

a woman, plump and silky as mozzarella,
lowers her buttocks into the bath
    behind your pupils

if our burly super,
    percussionist of pails,
    boiler-master,
grunts a greeting,

you—suave native male—pause
to exchange crumbs of small talk

like peas thumbed from a pod, sparrows
    bounce round your feet,
hungry

Down the Hall, the Bookman

withdraws the heel of his palm
from his long chin, unfolds slowly,
sways
rising to grasp the gape-strawed broom
to sweep shells and shadows aside,
until a passage,
the width of a foot,
snakes between boxed books
and piled disks
ringed with melodies

when the record player fixes itself,
he'll play the old songs,
from musicals

a long ago curdles in his veins
violin strings tug him, dozing,
past eddies
no arrows here
there's only one way to go—
through programs
            magazines
            librettos

he shifts,
sorts
no room for customers   few come
the radio never stops going

the bookman's hard to topple
when he's up
though he shuffles and staggers
and spills his cargo
and taps his forehead, mumbling
'empty' and 'bird-brain,'
exposing his mastery
of affectionate self-deprecation

a stray,
eager to crowd in
with his long ears
to take coffee, use your phone,
he'll get his place straightened out
sometime soon—
one of these days

for Herbert Oxer,
in memory now

Master Fashioner

"I could never take a ruler to measure a thing in my life. . . .
I think the ruler is in us."
—Louise Nevelson, interviewed for *Vogue*

this gold eagle's wing, that tusk . . .
caught when they fell away

plunged through the skin we call reality,
I grasp what I need, surface
with tools for new alchemies to shelve
in moonlit vestries

climbing my own shoulders, I in-
form each edge until it fits, turn
even the banisters   I say the ruler's
in our spine   grand gestures suit me

a foot is how it feels
striding through my empire, I shine

In a Museum of Contemporary Art

when, having taken too much wine with lunch,
they looked around thinking "art"
then, gazing (as one gazes at art
in a museum with marble floors—
from some distance) at the two man-size
apothecary jars flanking the crate
shaped like a coffin,
each in his time approached,

tilting to hear the whisper
of art, feeling a bit high
not one of them ready
to take personal stock, being at the moment
with the elite few come to examine,
to recognize, or reject
"art," peering down-in, when

behold! an actual woman
dead? at rest? with what object
on her chest? and, in a tangle around her,
loose loops of exposed film,
a gelatinous evergreen blackness
each heard *click*

each, caught in the face
of a minute's shutting, awoke to . . .
no no, not yet!
after all we have been through
not to be just sentinels, cedars,
apothecary jars, putting our arms
around each other to keep
the connections close, doors open,

to make ourselves art also—
chronic objects of examination
with our rich histories—corked,
but transparent to everyone else,
upstanding lovers in our sensitive skins
was this a joke? and where
are they now, those jars

Stopping the Arrow to Weigh Its Flight

inflamed spring comes suddenly in playing purple
    and deep-yellow notes
along gutters crushed cellophane sharpens light
two suspects comparing bright ties on Wall Street
    show teeth in unison

the urban body-politic continues to suffer boxes
    gates steps
continues to line up in chorus or at the baseline,
to engage with buttons and lovers, to growl
    at the specter of a strike

on a fire escape in Chinatown, fish flap beside
    the kids' underwear
flanks quiver under a kitchen sink when, far off
    on the molten pewter of the sea, red stacks hoot
    reminding prisoners they can plunge
    and swim for it
pistols appear in the fists of children who uncoiled
    squealing party-tongues last evening

yesterday, holding an umbrella over us, you leaned
    to kiss my pigeons
today a crimson bird hurls himself against my window-
    glass, his own rival
a man chews his vanishing dog watching breasts bounce
    under blouses
say! let's have dim sum this Sunday, whatever
    the weather

seeing his son off, the father lifts his hat
under it, a nest, a root of flight
two oranges touch on a polished table
one whispers rumors of oases and horizons
and a howling metro drains from the station—
    a boy's face pressed against every pane

You Don't Hear Me

you chatter holding me away
from chores that must be wiped daily with a wet cloth

you go on   like a spider spinning high above
    dry urban sluices
where politicians pile ice-cube promises in heaps
    on summer corners
and a red rose from a typist's scarf dreaming of Paris
    sails away at eye level
through air just beginning to congeal into a pumpkin

I tried to tell you about *The Wall* but couldn't
because you put your foot in my gate
    and kept it there,
describing the bustling Hasidim tucking side curls
    under black hats,
painting for me how nomad winds
    ballooned the skirts of wigged women
    so they rose and were scattered,
and how a clutch of them were carried all the way
    to China and dropped on a pug-dragon's broad back

it was at that point an obese queen of Hawaii, torn
    from my book of travels, came to mind—
    a cigar between her teeth, fruit piled
    around her throne—a powerhouse!

I anticipate pale hours digging
    in the cloud-mine of words,
over woods I've walked through, red-hooded,
    with crystal syllables in my basket,
    envying the hen and the pastry cook

right now I'd wolf anything down
but you keep tooting, clacking your lips,
until I'm forced to grab at moths escaping your
    kettle's spout—the dark ones,
not bad tasting, like bitter chocolate

you go on and on—insistent as a cicada,
while even now in the southwest a tumescent sun
 spreads yellow oilcloth on mesas
 and the goats begin nibbling in the valley
I breathe into a sieve already clogged
 with my internal fog
but you're chattering about a kink in your neck
so you can't hear the piper, his plaid
 udder underarm, marching slowly and stiffly
 through a rubbled lot, whining and yearning

do you remember the squeal when you swiveled
 the high stool at the counter, impatient
 for your shake?
and then the dizzying spin among migrating wings?

I'd like to migrate

I consider migration as you uncrate umbilical cords
 gathered last night in sleep's jungle
I'd ask if you ran into your deceased mother there
and if she hissed or purred about the accommodations
but I can't get a word in
yours crackle in my ear

your bakelite mouth is too close, at my ear,
as I look over the city's long teeth
 from my window
and watch morning's white scarves retreat

red and white sawhorses whinny and sneeze
 in the street
as candidates flow by—pepper in the wind

a red rose slips into a speaker's buttonhole
I can't hear him you're still talking

What I Miss, What I Want

splinters from wrecked childhood galleons,
knob from a cedar drawer, a lion paw
from father's chair,
the petite ring I wouldn't wear,
grooved shards of Caruso

but no,
surf retreats with its full load of detritus

only ephemera, Ideas humanity has courted,
    slept with,
Ideas I have knelt to, head bowed,
    in the company of thousands,
wash up on the beach of my desk
like ghostly jellyfish

and lo!
before I can shape them to my diction,
they rise, draped in traditional phrases,
and depart,
each pompous as a lord : last words
    on the subject

oh for a dithyramb!

but right now I'd settle for something humble,
a small pearl from the gut—
luminous—
a Lorca-like lyric . . . about the cool moon,
    for instance

even kelp—black, elegiac—
(as long as it had a life of its own, mine)
or a quick crab to make the mind leap

I want more than one
. . . enough for a potlatch

I sit poised, prepared

2. i hear longing strings

February 8

poles are down   at the city's fringe
boxcars sleep under ermine   wind
shakes huge sheets

an arctic fox
pads invisibly through the street
tongue like a ship's flag

at sea, a fog horn complains
it's too far between hearts

that's why snow mice
huddle on sills
frozen milk slides
down dim deserted chimneys

at each corner a statue
clutches a cup of ice

it's too far to go
I miss your face on my pillow

on my bed a pale lizard lies
reading the ceiling's
simple page

a pipe raps
no . . . it's the blind widow
making her way

I Hear Longing Strings

the laundry I hauled home this morning over dirty ice
    was not mine
I must make the whole trip again
to find, no doubt, my fine sheets torn to petals
    loves me, loves me not

the old man on the bench beside me smoothes a used
    hanky, like a map, over his thighs
a lesson of sorts I suppose

the old man could be he

no, deep in a forest matted with twigs and nests,
somewhere in there,
    in the castle-fortress,
he sits as I saw him last, pipe bowl in hand,
    one leg crossed on the other,
observing events lined up like soldiers, in columns
    on large pages—
the march of time

but time can't be folded like laundry

the drive back, 35 years or so, would be tedious—
    roots and trunks blocking the road
and the weather gets worse as you go

those who were there battled, flirtatiously,
    for the brass key
after the scuffle, someone noticed there were
NO WALLS either side of the door
and just stood there, holding the key

. . . might have been me

whose cheap joke I wonder

from distant woods, the longing sound of strings

back then I twirled the mass of my abundant hair
    into a fist, so I could loosen it—
let it fall free to my waist, for him
who would not raise the drawbridge
    to let the tender pass

would he lower it over the moat for me now?

as to parting—it just happens
and if not . . .
one's barber will make the decision

Emptying the Bowl

thick men make walls with news-
smudged fingers   where are you?
are you handling papers?

batteries pick up everything
atoms ignore what they shape—
glasses you nest in looking out
what for? what shape   the wind?
listen—wind

is the blood of space
its sound can't be looked up
the pipe you smoked, is it cold?

words wait in the upturned glass
sometimes you fill with me too
sap rises in the pencil
the pipe you bit smokes
rubies in the stopped watch blush

not the ripe, not the firm
plum of that time, no
not the plum in your pocket

a page is the poet's bandage
soot settles there
this summer thick men make walls
like sponges some coffins swell
yes, let's drink to news

green ponds congeal
olives taste black and bitter
ah me too   me too

At the Bottom of the Box

they've wiped Clark Gable's smile
from lids on ice cream cups
now no one licks their full moon tops

on train sills, there's no soot
no soot smell
the sky's green and the window sealed

still I share sweat
with my circling mare   ash coats
her caparisons and my hair

when I reached for the brass ring
it stuck   but I bought a ticket
to the moon, for luck

tell the blind spaniel
that sniffs through the house
Schnozzola has left us, soft shoe is out

I'm down
with the last crackerjack
down down in the box

I grope for a prize
along the smooth bottom
up the smooth sides

Tasting the Stuff of Clouds

fog is passing through
remove your hat please!

the lowing of old locomotives comes back to me
I look for owls
I look for Verlaine hiding behind his translucent smoke
  in a Paris café, one knee crossed on the other
iron stems hold up the glow of blurred bright thistles
Dickens strolls by, pudgy fingers rubbing his
  pocket watch
and Whistler, under his broad black hat, leans
  in a doorway near the pier

fog is passing through
and because fog is a polygamist it marries steam—
  steam privy to secrets of the underworld
agents, faces pale as frosted glass, slip past
  mouthing a code for the deaf
a small wind wafts it to lips dusted with plaster,
  lips moving silently in a palm

fog is passing through the waving hair of a gentle,
  elderly man brought home without his hat
its white webs embrace a plump woman bending over a bag
  of soiled clothes
fog, imported from a town on the tip of an inverted cone,
  a town with cobbled streets, a mountain town called
  Erici, is passing across this page

rescue workers transport three fog-wrapped bodies on sleds
  to the Museum of Natural History
I have seen a tall three-masted schooner emerge
  from a fog bank
at dusk fog makes opals of shop windows

it licks a dull sea-smoothed stone on a sill
    to a satiny penguin blackness,
    paying homage to its opposite,
adoring the stone because it is self-contained,
because, in the stone's untouched heart, dryness reigns,
    and gravity,

because a seed of crystal is enthroned therein
    and about crystal fog knows nothing

Evening with an Hourglass

the hero hangs on the ropes
considering the destruction of his nose

there's scarcely any living left among
the brutally stubbed in shallow dishes,
ashes of lost friends,
lost a second time in the plump
bag tied with a twist outside the door—

ashes, common as grains in the hourglass

coats worn napless shoved under seats
at the theater consult their folds
as though they could stretch into wings
to open and close—scissors
cutting shadows from light

the Book of Feeling
yields only a diminishing white pulp
worth no more than the scissor blades
vanishing in the wind—a night wind
that sleeps in the black bag
with ashes—

ashes like grains in the hourglass

one cone of it emptying down
to the inevitable sleep,
the other filling with limp silhouettes
cut by scissors too loose
to snip the wasp-waist
with its fine flow of sand
leading through sleep and out again
until the glass is broken
like the nose of the hero—

and we run out of ourselves

This Cigarette Could Be My Last

inhaling shallowly I watch shades
    shift in a tranquil cloister
once I stood on a boulder facing the cook
    with a hail of newly baked speech

children dig for clams past the fireweed
the organist must be hidden over the sea's
    far edge
for too long it's been Sunday
my knees ache

I've consulted the snake in the woodshed
    and a crow,
lifted the hen's wing, knocked on her eggs
    to induce dialogue
now I'll question the wise carp
why can't I breathe?
who blew notes from their cables?

I unfold my hanky
a darning needle escapes to mend distance
I recall how we paused on a pier under sky's
    bright lens . . . and your warning
nevermind

sighs trail like soiled gauze from a wrist
    bandage
with a cat curled on my thighs, I could watch
    shades shift for eons
but I'm driven to follow the salmon upstream
    to connection

elevate my knees
try mouth to mouth resuscitation
I've been inhaling shallowly too long

Untitled

heart, come from the woods, if that's where you hide
in poison ivy or among royal ferns
I've returned from sleep with purged eyes
here's the clean bowl of my self—
bone cage, flesh of clay
without me you'll be served thin soup in a tin cup,
won't own even a sooty sill to rest your elbow on,
will be nameless, without herd or pack, with nothing
except longing and a muzzle full of quills
to remind you of murdered birthdays

all night love letters blew down my corridors
brushing against each other
all night I chased them out the back door
and watched as they careened like loose petals
through the field where long grasses scratched the sky's belly
and sometimes called to them not to come back
and sometimes sighed with relief
and sometimes wept as I watched them turn into mourning cloaks

heart, come home now
moist and wild as always, you'll fill your central place
but first I want to hold you
I need to warm my hands—
my hands are very cold from the journey
one night, cast down by separation,
you'll shrivel and darken
and warm me no more

On the Long Fall Down the Vault Steps Stopped

Turned by the *thump thump*, struck
by the sight of her, supine, by her silence—
she who rained me out once,
she whom I mother now, puddled
on the leveling floor with legs angled up,
wide-eyed, addled, not yet horrified
at having been urged earthward,
at having let go—brittle column collapsed. . . .

Oh rise, rise jessant
as a spring, rise as a sprout from the cross-cut,
the axed heartwood, the stump
left from what planked my child-bureau brushed
with spring green, rosebudded with sealing wax,
in whose stuck drawers we pose, caught
in emulsion, curtseying in Kate
Greenaway calico dresses among balsam pillows,
among dried flowers, matchbooks, petticoats.

Rise as a shoot from the root-stock of rosebush,
winter indignity over. Grow, branch, bud
to be plucked again, pink satin indulgences
you adored, for the gray chiffon
loosened in waltzing, in being turned.

Stop. Don't be blown
open. Don't petal down, don't.
What we in living did, we must undo—
our nots, knotted by us (if not by us, who?)
as we shrink, as we trip into fall.

Mourning Raga for Hannah Tillich

they tell me you fell
back straight, in love, I suspect,
with forgetting . . . let self drop

like a pebble   rings intersect
as we lift cooled glass-rims to our lips
pooling clues to depths touched with you,

who, at the end, would not run old film
past light but sat, nest-bound,
behind panes watching shade shift,

watching each day slip into the wedge—
geese winging through autumn blues
you too wished to fly from

outside, a tree stood in its puddled
red leaves   inside, the white cat
stretched his throat on your thigh

sealed in granny-skin, your red-
riding childhood won't return
from the woods, from the dim gullet

now your breath spreads through foliage
away with age, with passage! yet,
though death tossed you high,

you're here in this book-bricked house,
mischievous, curious, sharp-
nosed, intent on looking direct

into pockets for our changes,
bells, threads—points you'll grasp exact,
prying knots open, even your own, in

lines scratched on postcards, notes
in migration, crossing mine
I see you small, embossed on blue—

Hannah, in a new straw hat,
straight-backed, trim,
waving from a bridge to us

who are fingers from your time

It's Always Then Now

In memory of Cynthia Lasky
Taos, New Mexico

far off, on the unending sentence of a southwest road
you approach
swinging hips, parentheses

it's sundown

the shadow you cast almost touches my toes

cuffs flap loose
around soft fingers wrinkled and stained
from peeling plums   reduced   made sweet for us

a leash swings
the black retriever runs loops through crackling fields
or leaps at your side

you will not arrive

I must learn you again—dressed, as then, in the shaggy
jacket Taos wears through fall . . .

learn you by heart

neon-red clouds descend to the Sangré de Cristo's
coal-black foothills

sunset's mass proceeds at a solemn pace

still you approach me

then (suddenly) this cheek of our globe turns from light
and you fade

Moon's Wife

I poke sleep's granite egg with my stick
but, love, you won't be born to me as body
again, though breath enters the beak
of the pelican and I pray with the pelican
when every act is prayer

on the slope of Ubeda, a gray olive tree
bears your cool eyes through summer's oil
and autumn dryness   it is not
you   beech buds, red shuttles in the weave
of atoms are not you

flamingos in the zoo
in their fenced-in green with the small
stream we waved across, have forgotten
that time of shores when you waded
when I waded   when we carried binoculars

oh have you forgotten our time of shores?
you, who died losing your self in red rivers. . . .
birds spill toward the sea   now my upturned
palm tests the precipitation

today the sun, rubbing Earth's pewter
kettle, summoned all permutations
of you but the all-at-once   I can't name
that armada of ducks in the distance

at dusk, lost where fears and conceits ramble,
I seek at least your glove that stroked
the dead flicker's feathers, and find
I'm the moon's wife who at last knows
what she lost—unlike the seasons,
you were born to me once only

Close Call

in a room papered with war, the telephone rings
a circle of numbers drifts toward the ceiling

I close my hand on the black tongue
babies with open mouths ooze from the receiver

a voice from the grave staggers—your voice

a paper rose sprouts from the receiver
the smell of mold, feet, urine,

an ocean slipping

from the receiver's sieve something green
delicate as lettuce—

something clean—falls to my lap
what the sea left on your brain

its whiteness love

3. time shared

A Snowflake in the Eye

no need to carry meaning to us in pincers
or put the sailor into day's bottle

yesterday climbs back through the porthole
bringing no more

than a cargo of weightless blossoms
bursting slowly
into their names : pink dogwood, for instance,

programmed to bloom on call behind the eyeball
even at sea, as you've just seen—

figments of the seasons' durable return
like snow

we have so little
time to share—

you loan me your binoculars
your horizon drops to my eye level   even so

there's my candle-bud, and yours

Between Home and Home

Naples, 1951

waiting for the passport you lost you walk
crossing the bridge
where he first saw you (slim then)
on your daily stroll with your aunt
he mute in khaki   wanting   aching to reach
each day. . . .

approaching at last
bridging the gap   respectful   with flowers
and a mumble of foreign sounds

on that bridge now—plump brunette
in maroon with fur collar—you reach
for him : your husband in Fairbanks
here there's a cathedral the color of caked blood
bells toll   remember snow
light a candle at the consulate   wait

for them to replace your passport
how long has it been?
unsnapping a folded yardstick
measure one winter tree by its shadow
step up to a stranger
say something American   something sad

together count minnows flipped on the esplanade
men bend over nets
imagine your passport trapped in the deep suspense
minutes crease the bay—wavelets
presently you are missing . . .
missing husband   child   home

bridging the gap
moving along now   counting back
forty below   a blackout
through the night you hold . . . you held
your infant to the heat of your breasts—
the infant you made with him

it's night in Naples
unfold the bay   smooth it
without a doubt call up the moon
watch it rise   believing
button your coat   step out on the platinum
moon-road   to Alaska

Behind the Old Woman's Dark Glasses

Vence, France

the countess's hat has brimmed on a head of wind
from the top of her stone wall,
or it slipped, to tease,
into the dusky slot behind a couch—
tired of defending against sun
hiding to be sought

she claims it has been kidnapped by a spy

on her bed table an empty jar
holds a few regal drops—Oil of Swinburne
to smooth politics between stars
thick as olives on the contorted tree

yellow stitches across her collapsed chest
diagram the constellations   more than one
continent kissed her feet,
her hand, her crest   the hat has blown off
with zinnias and roses into shadow

behind the dark glasses she wears, a spider's
spinning motor draws rumors—
thin as spittle—across the valley-troughs
filled with appalling space

imagine, at her age, she eats everyone!

can you smell her sizzling lamp above Vence?
or hear the piano from old storms moving
in the cypress thicket that screens the tank
where ancient carp float in a half doze
waiting for flakes she has forgotten
for days to feed them

she lifts a plump fig, a Europe sown
with the larvae of discord, from the bowl
she has eaten it again and again
but it's too late to totter alone
with flashlight through the cool weeds

night's victimized in her : a squealing rat,
an abandoned infant,
or a ghost caught in leaves of a nut tree
tugs her to the balcony   far away,
below, the moonlit sea resonates

from across it, a dawn breeze—a whisper—
promises a young sailor with blue eyes,
a Mozart, a Goya, bringing her broad-
brimmed hat back to her

Short Story

but not before four! he stirs the first
with his finger   he has forgotten his address
but returns to brick and insists
on windows and dramatic exits
in a space without walls where any vein
could be followed to the light source

he came armed with a wound
begging in a foreign tongue   but sometimes
by certain tender acts at night
crossing thin ice, he seems
to lead her to understand . . .
he suggests . . . there's a promise . . .
already she tastes the sea

a frigate bursts from her chest
he hooks it back
but doesn't himself keep track
and won't recognize detours, old waterways—
habits engraved in quartz   he pours
the first drink at four and demands

she give him a hand
she cuts carrot sticks for him   but not
the right way—his way   his ache spurts
his fist flattens a mosquito
at bay, she could weep   but doesn't
ears deep in her brain become his librarians
he wants her being

holding her city to his ear, she tells
him a dream : someone released from prison
an old child, walks a road
between Lombardy poplars with a red
wagon in tow   the arm in it grows
heavier and heavier   *turn, grieve*
and bury it she tells him   *I know*
I am not that arm

she cuts his meat in small
pieces but he's *not a frigging swallow!*
his chair rasps the floor and falls
sliding a dollar under the plate
for the waiter, she leaves too
above the high buildings, the sky's sea—
twinkling with a billion minnows

With Your Breath

to Michael Burkhard, poet

even as you pull a thread
from water's cloth guiding it through your pen
making little snarls

a tree springs up from the page

and fades
ready to rise again before my eyes with you
in it, protecting your tree

from ax and highwayman

perched there under a hat, pen
tied with string to your navel, umbrella
hooked on a limb,

you half doze among apples

in the canal below, ducks
paddling among model boats, strike at crumbs
from a loaf

with distance baked into it

there goes a crumb
through the silver circle a windmill makes
with its whirling blades,

drawn beyond fixed channels

beyond water
to a crypt near nothing, and nowhere, in the cold
bubble of space   but here

you cup an ear for the flow—

love and longing : ripples
your breath engraves on tablets of fog
set so close

not even death can pass

When Asked How This Drawing Series Began, He Said:

in the outback, far into rocky wild land,
past an abandoned mine, then human hands
    outlined on a cliff-face,
I found a small circle of stones around
    smoothed dirt

for prayer? fire?
the fact of intent struck me—

witness to the presence of early men like us,
    and yet not

a minimal displacement . . . rocks from the site
not smoothed, not hacked
equal in function, but each formed by its own
    crystal code

retracing my route, I explored the mine's
    wound : rust-crusted cables, gears, rods,
noting how weather intercedes to reclaim tools
    from imposed smoothness

once home, arranging a stone wreath, I voiced
    primal sounds,
tasting stored potency as each syllable climbed
    from silence

with pencil I drew hands near a few stones
    from the circle
next, an ax—
    wooden shaft
    chipped stone wedge
    vines joining them

here, below a horizon line, the ax again
    imbedded in rocky soil
    handle down, phallus-like

or, as in this sketch, up . . . sprout
    from an ax-seed—invention
scratched with graphite on a surface
    once tree : pulped, bleached

rock circle, mine ruin—my thoughts leap
    between them
I haven't yet come
    to the end of possibilities
on each page, the residue—
    enclosed, (liberated?) energy

and still that first flash haunts me:
the placement of small stones
    in an approximate circle—
imprint on nature by man,

on man's creations
    by rain, wind . . . God's hand?

for Martin King, Australian artist,
whose series it is

The Redon Boy

something humped in a corner stirs
something in silver fur
goblin bats, swift as thought, whisk
through passages in his skull

if he puts a foot on the cool floor
the night-queen's nacreous hand
may clutch from under the bed

that creak—could it be
rocking springs on a coach
behind four restless horses?

he tiptoes to the window

in the pasture a fresh sadness
gleams on Earth's lashes
moon-water foams, heavy in the pail

if he drops over the sill,
wading a dewy trail
through night's hushed pupil
to the garden's brocade,

he may find a coach
waiting for him, the boy Odilon
(who plans to achieve great things on Earth

with his marbles, his kites,
his pocketknife with five gadgets),

a coach to speed him to the moon—
the glabrous moon who scratches her side
on the oak's forks,

who even now tugs at her cords
ready to sail—white as camphor—
into a paling sky

Bearing His Stars

for R. Peters, poet

he runs naked
in thin mountain air

redwoods flash by, then dwarf pines

a brass skull with garnet eyes
raps his breastbone   his toes
touch the edge of snow

how high must one go
to fall?
is it called soaring then?

below, a child lies,
his child
whose death shrank history

he sees his flayed years
strewn in the valley

where love should be
he knows the amputee's pain

yet he'll transfix us—ripped open,
guts steaming, he'll parade

and when his skull breaks
from its chain of vertebrae?

his blood-gems—compressed,
explosive, light years away—

must shine

To Be Borne Again

her confession

because the religious cow sneezed on me
as a governess would sneeze on a derelict and I fled
leaving the barn door open
irritating my father,

his fat condensed into seven candles
and his eyes flamed when I came in late Friday
with a shawl over my head to hide tears large
as my budding breasts,

because my tears are the Ottoman's pearls
yet he will not drop down so I can sit on his back
sniffing the forbidden poppy watching the world
go bye bye,

because worlds go on, meters ticking,
though company mice are no more to my liking than cows;
to be nibbled is not better
than to be cropped,

though crops this year were ruined by the queen's reign
proving that, elbows or no elbows,
she's unstable as a cloud

because, these days, even children claim territories
and throw sandpies as though anyone but the ocean
owned the beach, now littered with elbows
tears locks and limp mice,

I'll slide into darkness where Queens and Ottomans
are the same as anyone, where nourishment goes down
without chewing, and the water's warm,

to be borne again, flung over Earth's shoulder—
field of grain

Widow Road

Vence, France

her son has deserted the chair by her bed
the dog digs holes in a mountain's shadow
a lizard slips under her roof tiles
he knows there are no ordinary roads

if she knew where to cast the rope
grief would pry her hand open
and the drowning self would save her

wind sweeps the descent between stone walls
small lights blink on the next mountain
she measures night's field by its bright motes
since sun dropped in the valley's basin

her right hand pinches the flame
her left relights the candle
a folded sail balanced on her head, the widow
descends the steep road to the sea

but wind has gone home
leaving grief so deep so wide, the dead man
drowns again

A Wilderness in the Veins

Taos, New Mexico

at the window, she watches sun's
bright ball dance sweet-foot
down sky's corridor

words have taken the path his boots wore
yet something of him arrives . . . an invasion,
an itch—sharp, like a sting—
from a crack in decades of dried mud

at five his boots scraped the doormat
then the sharp *rat-a-tat*
he slipped in, chuckling,
made waves, laughter,
mock-skittish gestures

he brought scissors to snip shadows,
swivelled lamp necks,
drew or parted curtains
expostulating about light
complaining about the smell of garlic
he took a bourbon, then another

in the yard winter trees wait
like upright forks

yes, something of him drifts in
with dusk from a high desert—
that wilderness in her veins
where small fires cool swiftly

Sketch of Tilli

Taos, New Mexico

short and brittle, Tilli stirs
bubbling green plums

I don't never go out now
doctor says not to
here, taste this
I lean toward the spoon
can't read . . . mustn't bend

from a step-stool Tilli reaches
between bead-bound Marys
and children framed in filigree,
to lift down a figurine
proudly she winds the key

a porcelain ballerina, en pointe,
in her porcelain tutu, revolves
to a slow pebbly-sweet melody
now, ain't that pretty? she prompts me
yes, lovely, I lie

sampling beets, relish, pie, I glance
outside   jeans, extra large,
pegged to the line spell BIG FARM MAN
bear waist, bear hands

her eyes follow mine
he's out she declares

I know   his truck door slammed
tires scrunched gravel
the cloud of dust in his wake
settled, before I unhooked my door

he's out, she repeats, this time
from a room off the kitchen
where she sits at a cot's edge,
swollen legs dangling

it's my heart, honey-dear,
can't lie down for the fear
never marry she warns *never!*

now I'm off, arms filled
with tomatoes, squash, corn, preserves,
more than I hunger for
bless you she calls

I half turn, see her dwarfed
on the door's dark page, raised palm
lined like a cross-section
of cabbage *God lover you!*
and never . . . you hear?

Offering

She had come to dance in the meadow
on the board placed across a tub
shaped like a coffin, but they'd moved it
to a field up north.

In a rough cabin redolent of men,
she rushed into a circle of his kin
in place of the girl who left him.

There had been no intention,
only the moon, its tides.

A crushed country hat shadowed his eyes
This tall young man with a temper drew her.
She said so.

In spite of his black spirit?
No, because of it. Smiling, cousins
winked to each other.

Eye to eye, she straddled his thighs,
slipped to the floor with him,
lay snuggled against his side,
his shoulder her pillow.

Would she cook, clean, sew?
She nodded. His sisters smiled.
They were all pleased,
a pleasurable spilling over.

In the yard, glimpsed through a window,
a crate made with fresh boards
shone in moonlight—
a crate too small for a woman.

And her inheritance?

The dancing board was old pine;
here a floor, earth under it.

From an uncorked vial, lilac essence
imbued the summer night.
Dark leaves, limp and dusty, hung
from a bush beside the cabin door.

Too late for blooms.

Still, in this woody, shadowed space,
the closeness. . . .

And the other—the girl who ran away—
where had she gone?

Was she dancing?

Letter from Indiana

for Carol Paiva
whose letter it was

yes, I think of him at times
like today   planting chrysanthemums
in the window box, I looked out
at hay in a passing truck
and thought : *his hay?*

there's football on local FM
I keep it on
the cresting cheers, the choppy voice,
keep me alert at the bindery

between innings, farm bulletins. . . .
I think of him then

I'm learning to letter spines
with gold leaf   it's tight work

when I get up, I'm stiff
it's too soon. . . . I've begun
to reassess my goals
I want a studio

tackling woodcuts at home—portraits
ploughed faces like peach pits
I'm getting the knack
it feels good to gouge

yes, I ran into him
a gusty September noon

at the bottom something stirred
sponge-full of what was soaked in
from our few meetings

between us, strange jumbled clues
dead leaves, in twisters

a spark? perhaps

I make too much of it

so little left

of fall   since then I've heard
nothing—
an austerity of choice

Letter from Connecticut

in memory of Richard Raymond,
whose feather began this

riding the ridgepole
lips firm on the nails
I glimpsed a flash   a few notes
struck me

dropping the hammer, I grabbed
the tip of a wing
shouting *give me the whole*
text from the beginning

when I opened my mouth, nails
sped down the roof slope
hammer after them

the thing tugged   I dropped
the shingle for a better grip
but, damn, it got away

I've a bright feather to show
a twig from the old elm Maggie says
but she helped me pick up the nails

last week the parson
wanted my poems
in place of the sermon

couldn't get through the door
so I read from the roof
airing the old stuff

most days
I don't get off the ground
maddening

all I want is a few lines
of sacred lyric

this antique machine
should be left to the flood
we don't understand one another

so be it
beans coming along
and a second grandchild

the neighbor took back his ladder
the roof stays up
Maggie's sick of the leak
though she's mending

In the Absence of Anyone

when night's wool wears thin
you can see a white moon
through the largest hole
and prints—small as commas—
where elk pressed ellipses
into its bright surface

arms reach through the hole
take the cool moon
toss it hand to hand
getting the feel of it
and the elk fall—

hands pitch it against the dark
but it doesn't return
it doesn't bounce back
though fingers flutter
calling it

it drifts like a paper boat
on a long gutter stream
until it's so small it fits
a dilated pupil
then the hole is woven over

elk fall like soot
in the alley where hands
pace up and down
hoping someone will come
to burn a hole in night's stocking

4. reaching for honey

We are the bees of the invisible. We frantically plunder the visible of its honey, to accumulate it in the great golden hive of the invisible.

—Rainer Maria Rilke

Communing with Myself

The Riviera, France

for once I hear the church bell's vowel
with my whole body

each hour drops, naked,
in the night sea

how seldom I retrieve day's offertory,

its shirts, sheets—covers of bed and bone
as they pour released from lines
billowing in white light

how seldom I realize layers:
violet shade on lemon skin,
juice in pockets, pith, Earth's
withering upholstery : prayers,

ringing my point on the wave

why not hallow shutters the color
of crysoprase in sun
pink geraniums on the sill
voices from a door—barely audible,
a stranger's flaking skin

why not requisition the sea,

the shuddering green behind these facades,
pine scent
delivered by the wind's postman or blue

glory blue
confined to morning notes on vines
climbing a wall

why not believe
in the penetrable shifting shadow,

in the eye—
resurrected daily
in the skull's chapel

why not believe a sleeping child's
curled hand by his cheek

or a fig
among dizzying leaves, then
a plump purse in the palm

why not in the mind's beehive believe,

in the communion of bees,
the queen as chalice   why not be
bemused with essential honey—

buzz and dance tell where to go

in the swarm find a fig's
solid weight

grasp it like a child, lift it, bite
through purple night

why not—now, after hours—
open an account with light
enter its flower

Anticipating the End of Distance

during discontinuous night
speaking a strange dialect
I arrive repeatedly
at a smooth depression   there
nose to stem scar
one can draw in the fragrance
of ripe melon snapped from the vine
whole and heavy

. . . navels equally near center—
yours, mine—it feels close
a way in, but sealed

deep in the numinous melon,
the womb of sound, seed notes
resonate with the enfolded whole
played out in time as we crisscross
a planet veined with routes
like a cantaloupe

if it were not for shrill midweek,
its making and dogging,
if it were not for this filigree of routines
on the skin, this filigree. . . .

yes but
slice in hand, mouth filled with melon
bitten down to the rind, yes
faced with symphonies of sundown,
gardens, Bonnard,
faced with harmonies between men
and women, or weaving airs
with someone dear. . . .

and then Bach's fugues . . . hearing them
as if the whole fruit were in me
and the stem at my ear

Is There Another Fruit with this Aroma

a woman calls from the moon—a hole
in the thick fabric of the usual
a man puts his glasses on and looks up
hoping she will see him   as though
the halo she wears like a straw hat
had a face

◆ ◆ ◆

it has a face
in your hands my cheeks light up
then night speeds inward to the dream hive

but now, by the river, I keep track—
watch boys patch a kite
    on a crest of sandy soil,
savor a small strawberry
    crushed between tongue and palate

who can count farina specks that stick
    to the pot as it boils over
each speck a moment
surrounded by outstretched hands—this
    moment : a seed of Being
lodged in my flesh

inside it, I take up the strand
    of a new name
follow its point-of-view to a country
    not my own

I'm you—as a boy—
holding a branch down
until father says firmly *it's alive*
    it will make flowers
I let it go

it springs
back   this moment I know your breath
    in my mouth
know how folded forsythia
    breaks through flute holes   each
sharp canary-note sprays
into air humming with bees

hands reach for this honey
can you leave
    without taking me?

Elegy

scarcely a breath left, running downwind
    to the enormous destination,
pierced deep, as thorns would. . . .

after hours spent digging
after struggling to cast off debris—
the backwash—your memories, mine,

until my vision sets in lightless space
where motes
    burn pinholes some call stars

old sounds return, laughter for instance,
having given up hats to spiralling wind
    in the black everywhere

(and me longing to reap forget-me-nots)

. . . with a little help, calling *so long*
into the monstrous absence,

wishing for the fragrance of sandalwood,

wishing to be by the Charles River, walking
    beside it, thinking of the Chardins
    I've just seen—a white pitcher
    and sun-drops on a white apron,

remembering your silver hair in sun,
sun on horse nettles in a field below eye
    level
where night's murders have been stamped
    over each other

faced with the grave's great seal
I strike it   with white flowers

Sleep Is the Place with No Knobs

when night draws out nails
    that hold the plot together
and cracks appear in thin ice
    on mirrors
where, in the depths,
    shifting selves dwell,

behind closed lids, a submarine
    surfaces,
its crew swarms on deck
rehearsed for love or war
    as the dream dictates

when, tucked in a pocket of space,
    the moon
shrinks to a coin
that would slip through a buttonhole
    in the nightwatchman's vest,

and the Trojan dream horse releases
    hummingbirds
inside high garden walls
    where stolen beauty blooms,

the sage of sleep plunges a hand
    down into his kimono sleeve
and extracts a fan
    spreading time's pleats

pale as plum blossoms, lovers
    peer from its dusty creases
toward the moist
    in common frontier of a kiss

there night's wedding cake gleams—
    a fortress waiting to be taken

but now, locked in the cast of Liberty
    enisled in the harbor,
I can't see a thing—

behind which open door are you hiding?

As Long As I Live

is it nothing to have ridden an animal before the wind
toward a goal one can no longer enter without effort?

goal—a long shaft with the sight of game at the end

nothing, at this time of year, ripens there
except light tricks
insight about some part
insight that sings, makes nothing, cleans

only a kick now and then, water from the nose
bending, or lifting a weight from the elbow

so I don't think I'm perpetual
though I remain at the crotch of distance
(a point always vanishing, as now),
walking with difficulty

or leaning against the frame at the mouth of the shaft
merely leaning, covered with sun
covered with blood or honey

I don't think 'nothing happens'
as long as I live
operating my vehicle with a driving head

or as a passenger—even horizontal at the bottom
of my boat—moving gently toward a goal
gently—that is, slowly, with awareness—
nothing else possible this season

descent of a weight : even softly hit,
a peach drops from its bough before ripening

lowered into a chair or the like (scale pan perhaps)
with a companion opposite, or at my elbow

or—windfall—an egg
falls from a tree to my lap
can't eat it by that time of course
nevermind

to move gently or gingerly, even lunging—
moving at least—

as a student of clouds, back
into reflection, the passageway, and around me
forktailed swallows coursing through
as though exiled from weight

closed doors either side

backstage,
where the eyepan can be found during the dying,
I crouch at the sight of game—flies
big as elephants, a trick of light through drops

drops, softly hit

the room is being,
at the bottom of the eyes

The Innermost Room

"I have often thought that the best mode of life for me would be to sit in the innermost room of a spacious locked cellar with my writing things and a lamp."
—Franz Kafka, *Letters to Felice*

in a mill, deep, where the wheels grind
awash in time, I'd penetrate
the faraway, the last cabin
on the road back, to be drawn

with smoke down the chimney to the room
where three little pigs giggle and jig
before the wolf-wind's huff,
to the fisherman, whose shrewish wife
demands *more more*

I'd watch water pour off hope
dragged up in knotted strings
. . . so much fear, tears also
but returning after all

scanning the diurnal azure,
my skylight-page, I'd follow
a tale about a lizard's love
how he willed wings
fumbling toward flight

how a gust shamed the strange scaled beast
but gave in at last
to the quest without end
for the wind's home, its ruby chalice

under my lamp's north star, I'd dwell
on a level with no support
inventing exploits against night
with a black pinion

The White Hour

in this silent hour measured by glass hands
the eyes of the elders dare me to move
it's freezing
the master raps his desk
yes yes but the route is traced in chalk on an icecap
I run my hand over my scalp   pawn?   queen?
men in soiled white bend over a skinned lamb
extracting pearls from its abdomen

in this clear hour measured by crushed glass
a bare bulb hangs from the ceiling
the doctor curving over me opens his fist
a confetti of winged buds rises
I'd slap them to dust if I could
but my eyes snap shut   my heart flees
I stick out my tongue for inspection . . .
misunderstood
and my hands . . . see   clean!

in this hour measured by glass beads
mother's fingers race on the ivory keys
where are you my steed?
a lion-footed armchair descends
astride its worn back I bounced to a Polonaise
but this wind has no sound
or the moist cloud I'm wrapped in

in this stillness measured by skeins of lace
snowshoes on my feet I'll strike out
for the place sweet clover quilts mounds
where green-eyed nurses in white
still come with full carriages
to eat lunch on headstones

I'll rest a wreath of burning tears on earth's face
blessing my horse's bones
blessing fingers and thighs
blessing petrified elders' eyes

in this hour of silence. . . .
how fogged glass has become!

I can't see my face in it
but there's nothing to fear   out there—
constellations   divinely indifferent
one star descends

in this smooth clear hour
why should I move across bare squares
why should I dare

The Headlight Through Us

I merely ask a bridge,
a mouth, an ear, this flesh—
the body transports

I ask merely space
and height without fear

to drive past the rift
and return, player,
to the body's instrument,

hand reaching or holding a bow
changing energy into pitch

imagine emerging from thought
not carrying freight, like light
from the prompter's box—

phrase from a score
existing beyond

but first a movement in the throat
emotion localized
floodlight on a night game

Rilke, say, calling the play
from the pit of his abdomen

I ask how it happens a human voice
bridges the white symphony of the sea
and we cross over

Your Path to Perspective

there's no point in arranging your steps to conform roughly
to an ideal circle
it's better to build an aisle to an event, ritual or practical,
at the apse of the horizon

don't ask if the wild land grows only rocks
just go—in your current constellation of atoms without
reforming the landscape, and

when the composer on the road lifts his head from his
instrument's belly where he listens like a doctor,
see if you trust the dream he draws out through his buttonhole—
shadowy woods where Longing with bitter-chocolate lips
crouches

here, in a clearing, the stone Venus wears a nest
where her head should be

if you believe the composer will sell his songs by evening
if you pass through him, having looked in vain for proverbs
among his leaves,

remember earth's passage through the worm
remember, though your eyes touch rocks in sequence, they are
all there always

down the road a young boy, folding slowly to one side
on a stone bench,
slips back to the bright grass

a small hand, white as plaster, severed at the wrist,
lies in shadow
rush to the lounge shouting soundlessly for help

if no one moves, even when a draft between door and window
sends a glass skidding on its moisture off a table edge,
remember how the boy clung to his granddad's leg
and how, when he shyly looked up, you saw a violin in each pupil

now you shake remorse from your fingertips thinking : against
whom, by whom, should charges be brought

and when you examine your own palm, don't believe in those many
    lines leading to the edge and over—
a sentence too heavy   one life suffices

you are where you planned to be, in a different place,
    watching

the woman carry her music stand to the evening road,
    take shears from her skirt pocket
    and construct a cage with staffs coiled on her arm

watch how winged seeds leave home migrating toward her extended
    finger

from now on, proceed softly down the road
you may hear a heart sing
                                        in your tongue's meadow

Night's Drownings and Resuscitations

nerves practice steadiness with spoonfuls of night
    before mind retreats
when drowning begins gurgles and gulps rise
    through tide's moving hair
a foot shoots out
victims lined up in hallways clasp x-rays of shrieks
    and sobs
the case could be terminal

parting silky eye-shells Death
    tests the ripeness of his pearls
a gleaming face presses against our aquarium wall
behind it black bands comb a red sky
high up Father of Dentists probes
    Moon's porcelain wiping the bees off
    on his starched white tunic
oh how Moon's roots ache on the dark side!

come! as cells in one body we must glide swiftly
    through gargoyles guarding the Dream Fort
    to hunt candles in night's wound
at the gong's sound
    portholes explode
    eels of longing slide from sills

all night strapped to sea's cabinet a woman's bones
    sit erect riding waves
she used to hoard green fire in her breast
will night's medicine restore wine to flesh?
will we ever again hear tall grasses hiss as they part?
where oh where has the tide taken us!

as the poet unfolds a dune heaves its sand
    toward him
boys press through thickets licking red sticky leaves
mamma leaps naked from the nest
a sculptor touches stiff cloth around a shape only begun
I can't open the chest I'm seated on

we must save ourselves! drag kidneys and lungs up
    through laminations of sleep   each of us   solo
    past roots sucking brown blood of fallen fruits
    past red herrings and dog bones
    past a beach of crushed clocks
until we taste day   see Dawn's goldfinch alight
    on a thistle

even now green lizard tongues unroll from lilies' mouths
sun butters coarse-grained earth bread
those doves lined up on a parapet may not be mourning
look! chirping grandchildren blow over the hill

Taking Off

"*The eye like a strange balloon mounts toward infinity*"
—Odilon Redon, title of a lithograph

show me your palm
I see paths, a bridge, the chapel—in its font,
    floating,
an empty smile

how many minnows in shoals will swim under
    the bridge tonight
as hearts, lifted and shuffled, experience
    turbulence?

maybe the smile will dissolve fear
as red knots drop from my needlework frame
    during takeoff

sliding my point through a hole
I pull the thread as far as it will go
reviewing how I began—walking into a widening

towards all those I've loved
on Earth, revolving and rolling in its fertile
    skin among the planets
thinking : when the pod bursts. . . .

thinking : soaked in night's ink, a floating eye
invites lost ones the way
a globe thistle traps wind